Welcome to Our Home

by Susan Buntrock

HAMPTON-BROWN

adobe
New Mexico, U.S.A.

beehive
Syria

apartment building
Hong Kong

houseboat
India

carved house
Iran

mobile home
U.S.A.

yurt
Mongolia

These houses have no windows.
Sunlight cannot come inside.
The houses stay cool.

These houses are made of clay.
They feel damp and cool inside.

This house has a pointed roof.
Snow can slide off.

Some homes are good for places that are hot and cold!

These houses are underground. The ground keeps the houses warm in the winter and cool in the summer.

Some homes are good for wet places.

This house floats like a boat!

This house stands above the water.

Some homes are good for rocky places.

This home is carved out of a rock.

These homes fit on the side of a rocky mountain!

Some homes are good for crowded places.

This house fits in a tiny space.

Many people can live in these tall buildings.

This house has wheels.

This house is like a tent.
It is easy to take apart.
A horse can carry it on its back.

Inside, houses are all homes.